# Lanzarote Travel Guide

*Attractions, Eating, Drinking, Shopping & Places To Stay*

Steve Jonas

Copyright © 2014, Astute Press
All Rights Reserved.

No part of this publication may be reproduced, stored in a retrieval system, or transmitted, in any form or by any means without the prior written permission of the publisher, nor be otherwise circulated in any form of binding or cover other than that in which it is published and without similar condition being imposed on the subsequent purchaser.

If there are any errors or omissions in copyright acknowledgements the publisher will be pleased to insert the appropriate acknowledgement in any subsequent printing of this publication.

Although we have taken all reasonable care in researching this book we make no warranty about the accuracy or completeness of its content and disclaim all liability arising from its use

# Table of Contents

**Welcome to Lanzarote** .................................................................... 6
**Planning Your Visit** ......................................................................... 11
**Climate & Weather** ....................................................................... 13
**Sightseeing & Attractions** .......................................................... 16
   **Puerto Del Carmen** ................................................................. 16
      Lava Flow Surf School ......................................................... 18
   **Costa Teguise** ............................................................................ 20
      Lively Lady Show Bar .......................................................... 22
   **Puerto Calero** ............................................................................ 24
      Submarine Safaris .............................................................. 25
   **Arrecife** ........................................................................................ 29
      Museum of International & Contemporary Art .......... 30
      Castillo de San Gabriel ....................................................... 31
   **Playa Blanca** .............................................................................. 33
   **Lanzarote Carnival** ................................................................. 35
   **Cueva de los Verdes** ............................................................... 36
   **Casa Omar Sharif (LagOmar)** ............................................... 39
   **Wine Museum** .......................................................................... 41
   **Timanfaya National Park** ...................................................... 44
   **Jardin de Cactus** ...................................................................... 45
   **Guinate Tropical Park & Penguin Paradise** ...................... 47
   **Jameos Del Agua** ..................................................................... 49

**Places to Stay** .................................................................................. 52
   Santa Rosa in Costa Teguise .................................................... 52
   Nautilus Bungalows in Puerto Del Carmen ......................... 52
   Lancelot Hotel in Arrecife ......................................................... 53
   Hotel Diamar in Arrecife ........................................................... 53
   Jardines Del Sol ............................................................................ 54

**Eating & Drinking** .......................................................................... 55
   Restaurante El Navarro in Costa Teguise ............................. 55
   TJ's Caribbean Tapas Bar in Puerto Del Carmen ................ 56

**Poppadom Indian Restaurant in Arrecife**..........................................56
**Atlantico Bar Restaurant in Playa Blanca**.................................57
**La Ermita Tapas Bar in Tias**.......................................................57

## Shopping .................................................................................................. 58
**Calle Real in Arrecife** ................................................................58
**Biosfera Shopping Center in Puerto Del Carmen** ..........................59
**Deiland Centre in Playa Honda** ................................................59
**Old Capital Market in Costa Teguise**.................................................60
**Casa-Museo Del Campesino in Mozaga** ............................................60

# Welcome to Lanzarote

Lanzarote is a popular holiday destination in the Atlantic Ocean and it is the fourth largest Canary Island (after Fuerteventura, Tenerife and Gran Canaria). It is located about 1000 km from mainland Spain and 127 km from the African coast. As a part of Spain, it retains an upscale, European feel. With 800 million years of history, Lanzarote is the oldest island within the Canary Islands archipelago. The easternmost Canary Island, Lanzarote is known for its widespread volcanic terrain (a tourist attraction in itself) formed by extensive volcanic activity in the early 18$^{th}$ century. In 1993, the United Nations Education Culture and Science Organization (UNESCO) protected Lanzarote by naming the island a biosphere reserve.

Lanzarote's native language is *Titerroygatra*, which means the *'red mountains'*. With crystal clear waters and an unusual moonlike volcanic geology, Lanzarote is home to some of the most unusual and startling landscapes on the planet. Because of its volcanic history, the island is covered with lava formations, and you may feel like you have stepped out of this world and onto the surface of the moon.

Between the dry climate and the lack of erosion, the landscape looks much as it did when volcanoes were active several centuries ago. The volcanic activity of the past few eons has created incredible craters and cave systems just waiting to be explored, including the longest volcanic tunnel in the world, the Atlantida Tunnel, which stretches over 7 km. During rare heat waves, the landscape appears blurred as dust from the Sahara desert carried into the island stains cars and houses and even affects people suffering from asthma.

Lanzarote's 213 kilometers of coastline make for stunning beaches with impressive views of the sparkling waters. For the more adventurous, Lanzarote's white beaches offer a variety of water sports from great surfing at Famara to windsurfing at Costa Teguise. The island also has great opportunities for snorkeling, scuba diving, canoeing and parasailing. Regulations regarding development have made sure that Lanzarote remains quaint and picturesque, with no billboard advertising and very few high-rise buildings.

On your visit to Lanzarote, some of the most enjoyable things to do iinclude stretching out on the beach, relaxing and dining out in a delicious seafood restaurant. Whether you prefer the excitement of Carnival or the quiet relaxation of the beach, Lanzarote is a favorite vacation spot to many who return year after year. And the small size of the island means you can enjoy its (often overlooked) sights without long drives.

Many think that the Canary Islands were named after the canary bird. But it was actually the other way around with the bird taking its name from the Canary Islands. The people of Lanzarote consider themselves more "Canarios" than Spaniards, and take pride in their strong connection with the sea-locked island.

Having been inhabited since 1000 BC, the island of Lanzarote has a rich history though much of it is now buried under lava or has been spirited away by raiders. The Phoenicians, Arabs, and Castilians have all claimed Lanzarote as their own, and in the 17$^{th}$ century, it was even raided by pirates! Today, the island is claimed by Spain and the population of 139,000 is mostly Spaniard.

The culture of Lanzarote is a unique blend of ancient traditions and European ideals brought in from mainland Spain. Place names are occasionally from the aboriginal language of the *Guanches*. Castilian Spanish is the national language, although the dialect and accent is closer to that of other Latin American countries than to that of mainland Spain. The population is largely Roman Catholic and religion plays an important part in the life of the island. Fruit and vegetable plantations can be found all over the island.

The island's main industry is tourism, with 80% of the island's residents involved in the industry in some way or another. Tourism, followed by fishing and agriculture, provides work opportunities for the thousands of locals and immigrants who come to Lanzarote in search of work.

Lanzarote takes pride in its cultural traditions. Traditional folk music is played on the *timple*, a ukulele-like instrument that has been played in Lanzarote since the 15$^{th}$ century. The *timple* is used at local fiestas accompanying dances like the *isa* and *folia*, and even the *tajaraste*, the dance that is said to have been passed down from the Guanches. Lanzarote also continues the unique tradition of *Lucha Canaria*, a form of wrestling where contestants attempt to throw each other to the ground inside a 12-meter ring.

Historically, Lanzarote has been a popular destination for artists and writers and the influence of these poets, novelists, and painters can be seen everywhere with several museums paying tribute to their works.

# Planning Your Visit

Located 127 kilometers off the coast of Morroco in Africa, Lanzarote is the easternmost island of the Canary Islands. At 60 kilometers long and 20 kilometers wide, it is the fourth largest of the Canary Islands. Even so, it is only about half the size of the U.S. state of Rhode Island. It is also the closest island to Spain, lying just 1000 kilometers to the southwest.

The powerful volcanic eruptions that took place at Timanfaya between 1730 and 1736 have influenced much of the landscape, although far more ancient eruptions have also left their mark. The Timanfaya eruptions of the 1700s marks the most powerful and long lasting period of volcanic activity in recorded history. Today, Timanfaya is a 51 square kilometer National Park entirely made up of volcanic soil. Though Lanzarote is small, the island has two mountain ranges: the 671 kilometer Famara in the north, and the 608 kilometer Ajaches in the south. There are over 500 varieties of plants and lichen on the island, and the harsh volcanic environment has caused many plants to adapt to life with a scarcity of water. Thirty-five types of animals live on the island, including one of two surviving populations of the endangered Canarian Egyptian Vulture.

The Lanzarote Airport, also known as Arrecife Airport, is located 6 kilometers southwest of Arrecife in San Bartolome, Las Palmas. Handling flights to several airports across Europe, the airport serves over 100,000+ tourists every year. Scheduled flights operate to other islands in the Canarian archipelago, to the Spanish mainland as well as to a few other international destinations. Some of the noted flight carriers operating from Lanzarote are British Airways, Air Europa, Iberia and Monarch. Local air carriers Islas and Binter operate local flights to other islands in Canary. A local bus serves both terminals of the airport – stopping at Playa Honda and the Capital of Lanzarote, Arrecife. Any further travel to other islands or onward destinations will need to be made from these two cities. Buses leave every half hour all days of the week except on Sundays when the frequency of operation is reduced. Bus schedules can be found at http://www.arrecifebus.com/index.php?lang=en

Bus tickets from the Lanzarote airport to the capital cost about €1 whereas the cost of a bus ticket from the capital city to Puerto Del Carmen is about €1.50. The taxi fare from the Lanzarote airport to Puerto Del Carmen is about €12-€25. The taxi fare from the airport to the resorts at Playa Blanca, down at the southern tip of the island, is about €30.

Once in Lanzarote, it is easy to explore the island in taxis and buses. Car hires are also relatively inexpensive and are the best bet if you are in the mood to explore the remote wilderness by yourself. From the northern tip of the island to the southernmost point, the island can be covered in 40 minutes. The east-west journey takes about 25 minutes from one end to the other. Because Lanzarote can get a bit windy in July, and make travel difficult, it is recommended that tourists avoid motor scooters and bicycles as these rides could be risky.

## Climate & Weather

Lanzarote enjoys a mild, dry climate year-round, making it an ideal destination no matter when you're traveling. With an annual average temperate range of 21° - 29° Celsius (70° - 85° Fahrenheit), Lanzarote enjoys eternal spring all through the year. However, the island has two peak seasons that experience a high influx of tourists – from November to April and from July to August. If you'd prefer to avoid the crowds and enjoy off-season deals on hotels and flights, the months of May-June or September-October are ideal times to travel. Summer rains are almost unheard of and Lanzarote experiences minimal rain, only about 140 mms, through the year. Favourable weather conditions have led to Lanzarote being tagged as the most fortunate of all islands.

You may also wish to plan your visit around one of Lanzarote's many festivals. If you'd like to catch Lanzarote's unique carnival, plan to visit the island during the months of February-March. *Dia de Canarias,* another unique festival, is celebrated the day the Canary Islands were granted autonomy from Spain, and is held on May 30th every year.

*Fiesta de Nuestra Senora de Los Dolores* is yet another indigenous festival that takes place in August or September. Locals dressed up in traditional attire embark on a pilgrimage to Mancha Blanca, the site of the last volcanic eruption that occurred in 1824.

*Dia Del Reyes* is celebrated in the first week of January, mostly around the dates of 5th of 6th. Three kings riding on camels throughout the island, distribute sweets to local children. Most of the festivities surrounding *Dia Del Reyes* are centered in Arrecife and Puerto Del Carmen.

The autumn months from September to October are also a good time to visit Lanzarote. Temperatures are warm and the northeasterly trade winds that blow through the island from March to August have died away. The waters of various beaches flanking these islands are warmer during these months making conditions favourable for swimming and watersports.

# Sightseeing & Attractions

## Puerto Del Carmen

The main tourist town on the Lanzarote Island, Puerto Del Carman is a part of the Tias municipality. With a large percentage of over 1 million visitors who visit the island staying at Puerto Del Carmen, it is no surprise that tourism drives most of the town's economy. Puerto del Carmen offers surfing, snorkeling, diving, and swimming at the beaches as well as a casino, shopping, restaurants, bars, mini-golf and several nightclubs.

Avenida de las Playas, the main avenue in Puerto Del Carmen, extends for 7 kilometers along the southern coast of the island. Beaches line one side of the avenue with restaurants, bars and shops on the other side of the avenue. Residential apartments, hotels and villas are located up the hill for about a kilometer inland from the coast. Puerto Tinosa, the harbour and docks are situated here. Puerto Tinosa hosts a number of restaurants that offer spectacular views of the harbour, land across the sea, the Papagoyan volcanic mountains, and views as far as the island of Fuerteventura.

With a number of scuba diving centers, surf instructors and dive centers, Puerto Del Carmen is a popular destination for all kinds of water sport activities. Cycling and running are also popular activities along the promenade and there are a number of bike hire shops along the coast. Average water temperatures range from 19° Celsius (66° Fahrenheit) in the winter to 23° Celsius (73° Fahrenheit) during summer. Average water visibility ranges from 25-30 meters. The international event, the Lanzarote Ironman triathlon is held on the promenade every May/June. While here, do take a tour to the Jameos Del Agua and Cueva de los Verdes caves and visit other sights like Mirador del Río and the Jardin de Cactus. With 4 levels of shops and bars, the Biosfera Shopping Centre is also worth a visit.

Most of Puerto Del Carmen's bars, restaurants and souvenir shops are situated within the New Town with the Old Town hosting several restaurants that provide spectacular views of the harbour, the marina and volcanic peaks in the distance. Originally a fishing village, the harbour is a beautiful place to visit has some noteable seafood restaurants. There are also a number of tourist shops selling duty-free goods, electronics, indigenous arts and crafts as well as designer clothes and shoes.

## Lava Flow Surf School

Puerto Del Carmen

Established in 2001, Lava Flow Surf School in Puerto Del Carmen is one of the best-known surf schools on the island.

The director and senior surf instructor has been surfing for over 20 years, mostly on the island of Lanzarote. Staff qualifications include Royal Lifesaving Beach Lifeguard, pool lifeguard, and International Lifesaving Society Surf Lifeguard.

Located in Puerto Del Carmen, the school does a daily assessment to decide which waves will best meet their clients surfing ability. They provide a safe and fun learning environment for surfing students of all ages and experience levels.

Classes are open to people of all ages and experience levels and they guarantee that students will be able to stand up on a surfboard and surf after finishing a course at the school.

A one-day surf course includes transfer from hotel/apartment to and from Famara Beach (pick up time 9 am – 9:30 am and return time 3 pm), surfboards and wet suits, surf lesson theory and practical, lunch on Famara Beach, one-on-one coaching, and a photograph. Cost is 40 euros per adult and 25 euros per child under 11.

If you're looking for more extensive lessons, the school also offers a 3-day course that also includes a Lavaflow Surf Lanzarote Merit Diploma. Cost is 110 euros for adults and 75 euros for children under 11.

And, if you're truly serious about surfing, the school offers a variety of weeklong camps. Accommodations are provided, in Eco Yurts, private apartments, or luxury villas, and costs run from 295 euros to 450 euros, depending on your package.

Lavaflow Surf School also offers courses in Stand Up Paddle Surfing, a fun sport that allows you to connect with the water and to stay fit. Stand Up Paddle Surfing consists of standing on a special surfboard and using a long paddle to propel yourself forward. Stand Up Paddle Surfing is not only recreational, it is also a form of transportation. Indigenous peoples throughout the world have traveled from island to island in this way.

Lavaflow Surf School also sells quality surfboards and wet suits, as well as other equipment. Their staff is available to help you make a selection if you'd like to invest in your own board and suit. For more information, call (+34) 636 39 15 49, or visit http://www.lavaflowsurf.com/.

## Costa Teguise

Situated on the eastern coast of the Lanzarote Island, Costa Teguise is 15 minutes drive from the Arrecife International Airport. Offering all different kinds of accommodation, Costa Teguise is touted as one of the most attractive tourist spots on the Lanzarote Island. A family friendly area, Costa Teguise's beaches, the serene surroundings and beach activities make it one of the preferred tourist destinations in Lanzarote.

Recreational activities range from a host of water sp a golf course and a water sports theme park. There are also several windsurfing instructors and schools along Jablillo Avenue and Cuchuras beach. Catering to all levels of fitness and expertise, these schools offer all required equipment as part of windsurfing packages. Running and cycling are also much liked activities here, the safe roads and the balmy climate making it a very enjoyable experience. The recent years have seen a marked increase in the number of sporting events and cultural events along Costa Teguise. Several events like the PWA Windsurfing Championship, the Costa Music Festival, and the Brazilian Music Festival are among the many cultural events that are held here.

One of the best options to explore Costa Teguise is to walk along the promenade, which takes you past the five main beaches on the island. However Costa Teguise's cooler, cloudier and windier climate make it a less preferred destination compared to other resorts in the southern parts of the island during winters. Costa Teguise's primary beaches, Playa Bastian and Playa Cucharas, offer a lot of good facilities like umbrellas and sun loungers, WCs etc. Whereas, other beaches like Playa Ancla keep it more natural.

While in Costa Teguise, do visit the only water park on the island. Only about 10 minutes away by walk from Pueblo Marinero, the Aqua Park is open daily from 10 AM to 6 PM. Half days passes cost about €18 per adult and about €15per child. Costa Teguise is also home to the only aquarium on the Lanzarote Island that provides a good diversion for families with children. Home to the oldest golf course on the Lanzarote Island, you can even enjoy an 18-hole experience on your trip.

...e has a quieter nightlife than its more alternative, Puerto Del Carmen. But there are quiet live jazz sessions at Jazz Mi Madre and there are a few nightclubs and lounges that are worth checking out. Additionally many of the resort hotels feature free variety shows in the evenings.

Costa Teguise has several car hire companies that cater to tourists on the island. Further information about car hire can be obtained here.
http://www.lanzaroteguidebook.com/car-hire

## Lively Lady Show Bar

Costa Teguise

Considered suitable for all ages, this restaurant in Costa Teguise is a comedy drag show bar consisting of comedy mime, live singing, and audience participation. Ranked number one of all the attractions in Costa Teguise, your visit to Lanzarote won't be complete without a trip to this cabaret.

Families are welcome to the shows, and the Lively Ladies bill themselves as "good, clean family entertainment." Karaoke sing-alongs take place after every show. You can even have a recording of your karaoke put on a CD as a souvenir!

If visitors are apprehensive, they need only read the reviews to convince them to take the chance and check out this show. The witty banter will have you laughing all night, and the music warrants standing ovations. The staff is friendly and welcoming, the atmosphere clean, and the entertainment top notch.

In fact, the shows are so good that many visitors return on a regular basis. Most visitors leave on first-name basis with the stars and owners. Costa Teguise is on the quiet side in the evenings, so if you're looking for a good night's entertainment, you can visit the bar every night you're in town. Since they do a different show each night, you won't see the same thing twice.

Shows start between 8 pm and 10 pm nightly and there's no entrance fee, although visitors are encouraged to grab a bite to eat or something to drink while watching the show. The drinks are also cheaper here than at most other bars on the island. Visitors should not that there are no shows on Thursday nights, although the bar is still open for your enjoyment. The Lively Ladies Show Bar is located in CC Calipso on Avenida de las Islas Canaries.

## Puerto Calero

Only a few kilometers away from the Puerto Del Carmen resort, the Puerto Calero marina is a world away in atmosphere, luxury and style. Located on the southwest of the island, the marina is only about 10 kilometers away from the Arrecife International Airport and 20 minutes away from the island's capital. In the recent years, Puerto Calero has become one of the most prestigious and exclusive addresses in the Canary Islands. Located on the outskirts of Puerto Del Carmen, Puerto Calero is a part of the municipality of Yaiza. Designed by Jose Calero in 1983, the construction of the marina continued for 4 years and was opened in 1989. On the 10$^{th}$ anniversary of the marina in 1999, it was extended to double its size to house more yachts. A super berth section, for boats 25-50 meters, was added in 2006. With 450 berths, the marina is now suitable for yachts up to 60 meters, and has housed some of the world's most luxurious yachts and vessels.

With two luxury hotels and a number of residential apartments and villas, Puerto Calero has been well planned with exclusive properties for sale at knockdown prices after the Spanish recession. The success of Puerto Calero marina has now led to the setup of other leisure attractions like the 75 foot catamaran which sets sail daily from the marina and sails along the east coast towards the Papagayo beaches and to Playa Blanca. You can hire a jet ski, sail on a catamaran or take a Submarine Safari, a unique deep sea experience which starts its journey from the Puerto Calero marina.

Puerto Calero hosts a wide selection of upscale restaurants, bars, and cafes with free Wi-Fi along the promenade and is a beautiful place to sit and soak up views of the million-dollar yachts. The marina has many stores that sell designer products and clothes, including Lacoste, Hugo Boss, Armani, and DKNY. If you are staying in Puerto Del Carmen, you can take an enjoyable walk along the coastal promenade to Puerto Calero and then take the bus or water taxi back home.

## Submarine Safaris

Puerto Calero,
Yaiza 35571
http://www.submarinesafaris.com/

Established in 1997, the Submarine Safari SL is the only true diving submarine on Lanzarote. Enabling the young and the old to enjoy the wonders of the sea, the Submarine Safaris have brought a whole new dimension to Lanzarote. Because pressure within the cabin is maintained equivalent to normal atmospheric pressure conditions, heart patients, pregnant women and people with ear problems do not face any discomfort. However, children younger than 2 years of age are not allowed on the submarine due to safety restrictions. Operating one of the most sophisticated submarine machineries in the world, the submarine is designed for total comfort and safety so that visitors can truly enjoy their dive.

Onboard the Sub Fun Tres, the name of the submarine, you are allocated your own personal seat in front of the submarine's huge viewing ports measuring 800 millimeters by 3 feet. The large viewing ports ensure complete viewing pleasure for every visitor. View ports also have their own personal TV monitors which provide the visitor alternate viewing perspectives, along with a display panel that provides continuous information about the submarine to the visitor onboard. The crystal clear waters and the diverse marine life around Lanzarote making the diving experience a truly unforgettable one. Onboard the submarine, you come face to face with huge 8 foot sting rays, angel sharks, barracudas and parrot fish in addition to three different shipwrecks which lie on the ocean bed. At about 80 feet down the trip, the submarine will be parked on the ocean bed. Visitors onboard the submarine get a chance to disembark the submarine, walk around it and click pictures. At this point, the submarine is joined by a scuba diver who performs an underwater ballet and hand feeds the amazing creatures of the ocean right in front of you, making the entire tour a remarkable experience.

Lasting for approximately one hour, including boarding the submarine and disembarking, each tour aboard the submarine includes a tour guide who provides comprehensive information about the submarine and the tour in German, Spanish and English. Cameras are allowed inside the submarine and high speed films are recommended to capture high quality shots. However, you should turn the flash off as the large viewing glass windows can cause flashback and white spots. Or, you can hold the camera extremely close to the viewing window.

The Submarine Safari tour guide is aided by extremely helpful staff members who will help answer any questions you might have about the submarine or the tour. A Submarine café and Shopping Centers display a large number of souvenirs and products where you can purchase mementos of your experience. The Café and Shopping center also doubles up as a Kodak express kiosk where you can get all your photos developed or get them copied on to a CD for viewing at a later date. If you have been onboard the submarine, you are eligible to a 10% discount on all products and photo developments at the kiosk and the Café.

The Submarine Safari website also has some interesting activities for children where they can log on to the website and try their hand at driving a submarine online. The Submarine Safari also holds colouring competitions every month where kids can download the colouring pages, fill them in and drop them into the Shark's mouth at Puerto Calero. The most recent development within Submarine Safaris has been the added operation on the Tenerife Island, providing you an alternate site of travel.

The average cost of a Submarine Safari SL experience is about €55 per adult and €32 per child aged between 2 and 14 years. The price of the ticket includes pick up and drop in Puerto Calero aboard an air-conditioned coach. Tickets can be booked at (+34) 928 512898 or booked online at the website.

# Arrecife

Arrecife is the capital city of Lanzarote. The word Arrecife means *reef* in Spanish, and Arrecife is named after the abundance of reefs and islets found along its coast. Located right in the middle of Lanzarote's east coast, Arrecife began as a small fishing village in the 15th century, growing until it became the island's capital in 1852. Today, it is home to around 50,000 people, nearly half of the island's population. The port of Arrecife serves several islands in addition to ships from mainland Europe and Africa. Shopping, culture, historical landmarks and the lovely city beach make this sophisticated city a welcome visit for the traveler to Lanzarote.

Arrecife is also home to two famous beaches, Playa de Reducto and Playa del Cable. With warm, tranquil waters and golden sand, both beaches are excellent locations for swimming and relaxation. A 2 kilometer promenade runs between the beaches so experience both by enjoying a walk in the sun. While in Arrecife, visit El Charco de San Gines, a man-made lagoon in the heart of the city. The Iglesia de San Gines, a parish church, named after the city's patron saint, is also located here. On the 15th of August every year as well as on Corpus Christi, the church becomes the central site of festivities. If you are here during these days, do not miss the events at the church.

Various plazas and parks are located throughout the city, perfect for picnicking or reading. If you'd like to take a break from the sunshine, Arrecife also has several cinemas, malls and restaurants. The nightlife of Lanzarote is centered in Arrecife, and an exciting selection of bars and nightclubs will keep you dancing until the small hours.

## Museum of International & Contemporary Art

Avenida de Naos, s/n,
Arrecife
Tel: (+34) 928 807 929

Housed in the 18th century Castillo de San Jose in the capital city of Arrecife, the collection is a unique and fascinating collection of culture and art. It's a modest but impressive exhibit, focusing on painting and sculpture. The building itself is a part of the exhibit. The historic fortress was originally constructed in 1774 as a center for the alleviation of hunger and poverty caused by the volcanic eruptions of the 1730s. As a result, it quickly became known as The Fortress of Hunger. In the years that followed, Spanish soldiers at the Castillo worked together to drive the British away.

Today, the museum's creation can be attributed to Lanzarote's own artist/architect Cesar Manrique. In the early 1970s, he persuaded the government to allow him to restore the Castillo building, and in 1976, the museum opened its doors to the public. The opening of the museum was a significant event in the country's history and the most ambitious exhibition held in all of the autonomous Canary Islands. With over 180 participating and invited artists at the opening exhibition, the museum now houses works by international artists, including Alechins, Bacon, Botero, Dámaso, Domínguez, Fráncis, Leparc, Millares, Miró, Picasso, Rompó, Tápies, Luis Féito, and the founder Manrique himself. It also regularly hosts temporary exhibits and conferences.

The attached museum restaurant is also one of the best on the island, featuring both international and local cuisines. The elegant seating offers spectacular views of the Naos port and the docks of Mármoles, and visitors won't be disappointed by the edible works of art on their plates. The museum is open daily from 11 AM to 8 PM. Admission costs about €2.50 for adults and €1.25 for children. The restaurant is open daily from 1 PM to 4 PM for lunch and from 7 PM to 11:30 PM for dinner. For more information, call (+34) 928 80 79 29.

## Castillo de San Gabriel

Islote de los Ingleses,
Arrecife 35500
http://www.spain-lanzarote.com/uk/places/castillo-san-gabriel.html

Located on Islote de los Ingleses, a tiny island within the archipelago, the Castillo de San Gabriel castle has an interesting history. Built originally as a wooden fortress, and equipped with only four pieces of artillery – one bronze and three cast iron pieces, the castle ended up being completely insufficient for any kind of defense, especially against attacks from the sea. Berber pirates eventually burnt down the entire structure. In the 16th century, the structure was replaced by a stone fort which played a crucial role in the protection and defense of the town and its harbour.

There are two different paths to approach the fortress – one that allows only vehicular traffic to go through and the other that allows only pedestrians. The pedestrian causeway passes over a drawbridge called Puente de las Bolas. Built in typical traditional defense architecture style, the drawbridge supports two huge cannonballs on top of its pillars and presents a formidable sight that takes you back to the historic era.

In 1972, the castle was declared as a National Historic Monument. The fortress also houses an archeological and ethnographic exhibit museum. The castle is often also used to conduct astronomical observations and related activities. Built within the tiny island, the fortress offers the tourist some exceptional views of the Castillo, the city and the Atlantic Ocean beyond. Local musicians often enthrall local and international tourists here lending a serene aura to the setting.

The castle is open to the general public only from Tuesdays to Fridays from 10 AM to 1 PM and 4 PM to 7 PM. On Saturdays, the castle is open only from 10 AM to 1 PM. The entrance fee to the castle is about €1.80 per person.

## Playa Blanca

Located at the southern tip of the island, the Papagayo Beaches in Playa Blanca are some of the best on the island. With clear waters and golden sands, you'll think you've stepped into paradise. Flanked by mountains and the mighty Mohana Raja, the beaches are sheltered from the winds and experience higher temperatures. A series of shallow water coves also frame these beaches and the town.

You can drive to the beach through the Monumento Natural de Los Ajaches National Park. Entry to the park is €3 per car. You can also take the Princesa Yaiza Papagayo Boat from the Playa Blanca harbor. This is a great way to see the sealife through the boat's glass bottom. It returns throughout the day to pick up those returning to Playa Blanca.

One can easily cover the entire town on foot and taxis are available. Walking to the Marina Rubicon takes only about 15-20 minutes while Playa Dorada takes a further 15 minutes. At the southern tip of the island, Playa Dorada is a short walk from Playa Blanca's town center. The water is clear, calm and shallow, making it an ideal beach for swimming, especially for children. Sunbeds and umbrellas are available to rent, and several restaurants and bars are within walking distance. Bars and restaurants offer low-key merriment in the evening. The Playa Blanca town center is another 15 minutes away. Taxis cost about €4 from Playa Blanca resorts to the town center. Buses are an alternative.

Playa Blanca has emerged as a resort for couples and families offering a quieter vacation. Because it is situated on the southern side of the island, the beach and resort are less windy than much of the island. The Playa Blanca promenade hosts a number of top quality restaurants and cafes where you can sample local and international cuisine, relax and enjoy the twinkling night lights from Corralejo's skyline on Fuerteventura and listen to the soothing noises made by waves lapping the shore. More information about the resort is available at http://www.playablancaresort.com/

## Lanzarote Carnival

Many people don't know that the island of Lanzarote has its very own carnival, but the celebrations in the Canary Islands are some of the biggest outside of those at the Rio Carnival in Brazil. The celebration includes parades, costumes, music, dancing, and food, and is a spectacle not to be missed. A time of riotous entertainment and revelry, the carnival provides an excellent excuse to escape from the monotony and daily routine and provides plenty of opportunity for fun and merriment. Normally coinciding with UK's school holidays for half term, the carnival's timing provides a good excuse to plan a trip to Lanzarote with your children.

The carnival is a public celebration that takes place just before the Christian Lent, and it gives everyone an opportunity to let their hair down a little. Because Lent falls on slightly different dates each calendar year, the carnival can take place anywhere from January to March. Confirmed dates on which the carnival will be held, are usually published online by September of the previous year. You can check online to find out when Carnival will happen during the year you're traveling. The website http://www.lanzaroteinformation.com/content/whats-lanzarote gives you a sneak peek into Lanzarote's calendar and shows a listing of all scheduled activities at any given time of the year.

In Lanzarote, Carnival festivities begin in Arrecife and then move to Puerto Del Carmen, Playa Blanca and Costa Teguise. Parades and concerts form the main entertainment with a multitude of dancers thronging the streets. *Murgas* are a popular part of Carnival. These theatrical and musical performers take advantage of the party to poke fun at politics and current events. A *murga* is usually performed by about 15 men and lasts about 45 minutes. It is a fun part of the *anything goes* atmosphere of the carnival.

A Carnival Queen is elected in a grand gala ceremony at the beginning of the festival, and much of the spectacle centers on her. The carnival also selects a Carnival Drag Queen. Both Queens get places of honor in the Carnival parade.

There are children's activities in the early evening in most of the Carnival cities. Some streets and businesses may be closed for the festivities. The party usually really gets going at around midnight and lasts until 6 or 8 am, so you may want to indulge in the local tradition of an afternoon siesta during the carnival!

Carnival has a theme each year so if you're planning on joining in the festivities pick (or make) a costume based on the theme. Carnival dates, themes, and other details can be found at http://www.lanzarote.com/carnival/.

## Cueva de los Verdes

Haria

Lanzarote's volcanic history has created a startling system of caves within the Monumento Natural del Malpaís de La Corona. The caves are roughly 3,000 years old, and are the result of eruptions from the nearby Monte Corona. The caves were formed when lava flows on the outside surface cooled and solidified, hardening into a solid crust as the liquid lava below continued to flow out to sea, leaving a tunnel behind. In some places, the tunnel roofs collapsed, creating individual caves. Upon partial collapse of a tunnel, the remnant structure called *Jameo* offers the tourist access to the other grottoes linked to the tunnel. Air draughts within the caves provide a natural ventilation system ensuring that the temperature inside the caves stays nice and constant at about 19° Celsius (66° Fahrenheit).

One of these tunnels, the *Tunnel of Atlantis* is the longest submerged volcanic tunnel in the world, stretching to 7 km. The caves also vary in altitude, stretching from 6 km above sea level to 1.5 km below sea level. The caves were privately owned until 1964, when a 2 km long pathway was opened to visitors. Today, guided tours are available through these caves and the famed *Tunnel of Atlantis*. A stretch of one kilometer formed by superimposing galleries with vertical interconnections between the galleries is prepared for tourist visits. Sophisticated lighting allows visitors to truly appreciate the beauty of these natural wonders. In some areas of the tunnel, there are three different levels which enables tourists to discover new spaces from different angles. While you are here, do not miss the awesome colours and the play of light on the vaults and along the walls of the cave.

The name *Cueva de los Verdes* means the *Green Caves* but contrary to their name, the caves are not green. Their name comes from their previous owners, the Green family. The caves are also famous for the 500-seat concert hall that has been created at the entrance to the caves. The tunnel houses two of the most relevant centers of culture, art and tourism - Cueva de los Verdes and Jameos Del Agua. If you are visiting in October, be sure to visit the caves for the Visual Music Festival. Organized in 1989, this civic event combines contemporary music with the island's natural wonders. Concerts take place in Cueva de los Verdes, as well as in Jameos Del Agua, Volcan Del Cuervo, and the Santo Domingo Convent.

The caves have a rich cultural history in addition to their fascinating geological history. Back when pirates and slave traders raided the islands, the people of Lanzarote hid in the caves to prevent capture. Be sure to stop by Jameos Del Agua while you're in the area. Tours through these caves are separate from Cueva de los Verdes, but it is well worth the trip to see the stunning underground lake. You may even catch a glimpse of the famed blind white crab, a creature unique to Lanzarote.

Located in the city of Haria on the northeast corner of the island, the caves are open daily for hour long trips starting from 10 AM to 6 PM, with the last trip at 5 PM. The best times to visit the caves are from 3 PM to 5 PM. The average price of the trip is about €9 per adult and €4.50 per child for children aged between 7 and 12 years. The fares are cheaper for residents of the Canary Islands. Local can enjoy the trip for €7.20 per adult and €3.60 per child for children aged between 7 and 12 years. For more information, call (+34) 928.17.32.20.

## Casa Omar Sharif (LagOmar)

Calle Los Loros, 2
Nazaret (nr. Teguise)
Tel: (+34) 928 940 064
http://www.lag-o-mar.com/

The inland town of Teguise is home to the famed LagOmar, a mansion once owned by the actor Omar Sharif. The LagOmar resort includes an art gallery, a museum, a restaurant and a bar and is well worth a visit. Originally designed and developed by Oasis de Nazaret developer Sam Benady, the house was intended to be a show home for individuals interesting in purchasing homes in the area. Omar Sharif, when in the area filming for L'Île Mysterieuse, fell in love with the home and instantly purchased it. But Sam Benady, knowing Omar's weakness for the game of cards and bridge, challenged him to a match where Omar Sharif ended up losing the game and the home to Sam Benady. Ever since the "one-day owner" Omar Sharif, left Lanzarote (never to return), the home has been called *Casa Omar Sharif*. Despite the house having changed owners, the current owners, Uruguayan architect Beatriz Van Hoff and German architect Dominik Von Boettinger have respected the style and nature of the space.

Set into the hillside, the home is housed at different levels and offers some spectacular views to the visitor. All through the house and the campus, you see several informative plaques explaining the history and displaying pictures of the home during its construction. With smooth white walls, use of natural elements like wood and stone and little pathways that lead the visitor through the gardens into caves, tunnels and through stairways, the house displays a lot of character. The campus also includes a water tunnel that has stepping stones built into it. The museum also houses a history of the actor Omar Sharif and his famed career. As a visitor, walking through the organic unique architecture, seamlessly integrated with the complex cave labyrinth makes for a very memorable experience. The chameleon like cave complex is considered truly exception, and touted by many visitors as a place that you would probably like to visit more than once, and yet soak in a new experience every time you visit.

Entry to the museum costs €5 per adult and €2 per child. Children 2 years and younger are admitted free. Remember that entry to the restaurant and the bar as well as the café is through the same gates that open to the museum, hence even if you only plan to enjoy a cup of coffee in the café, you would still need to shell out the entrance fee. During the months of summer, the LagOmar Casa Omar Sharif Museum is open Tuesdays to Sundays from 10 AM to 6 PM. During the months of winter, the LagOmar Casa Omar Sharif Museum is open Tuesdays to Sundays from 10 AM to 7 PM.

## Wine Museum

LZ-30, Km 11, San Bartolomé
CP 35550
Tel: (+34) 928 524 036
www.elgrifo.com

In operation since 1775, the El Grifo wineries are the oldest in the Canary Islands and one among the ten oldest museums of Spain. The buildings making up the winery were built over the lava remnants of the volcanic eruptions from the 1730s. Each building is made of volcanic stone and mortar, with ceiling beams made from the wood salvaged from shipwrecks.

Several-hundred-year-old tools and machinery from the winery have been preserved and are on display at the museum. Because of Lanzarote's remoteness, many of these tools were used for several decades after new tools were developed elsewhere in the world. Today, vertical hydraulic presses and stainless steel vinification equipment have replaced the equipment that is now on display at the museum. But the Moscatel vines that produce wine-grapes have been maintained since 1881, and the palm tree that presides over the estate is one of the tallest and oldest on the island, having stood since 1750.

Today, all of the work of the vineyard is done manually due to obstacles created by lava stone walls and several layers of volcanic ash. Every task, from grape farming to the bottling, is done on the property. Reaping a harvest of over 500,000 to 700,000 kilos of grapes every year, the vineyard produces 400,000 to 600,000 bottles per year, and has won numerous awards. The 61.5-hectare vineyard is owned and maintained by brothers Juan Jose Rodriguez and Fermin Otamendi Bethencourt, fifth generation of the two families that have owned the vineyard since 1880. Many of the customers who buy from the vineyard have been doing so for generations.

The volcanic soil is excellent for farming, but to lack of rainfall throughout the year and constant trade winds make it difficult to grow grapes. The workers of the vineyard have addressed these challenges by building protective walls of volcanic rock and spreading layers of lava gravel over the soil to prevent evaporation of water.

Guided tours are available of the wine cellar Mondays through Fridays at 10:30 am, and of the museum and vineyards Mondays through Fridays at 11 am. The vineyard also has a library of over 5,000 books on the subject of wine. Attracting more than 60,000 visitors every year, the wine museum of Lanzarote is one of the most visited museums in Spain.

The museum is open to the public every day of the year from 10:30 am to 6 pm. The entrance fee is about €3 for adults, and includes two free wine tastings. Prior booking is recommended. For more information, call (+34) 928 52 49 51, or visit http://www.elgrifo.com/en.

## Timanfaya National Park

Carretera LZ-67,
Tinajo 35560
Tel: (+34) 928 11 80 42
http://www.discoverlanzarote.com/timanfaya.asp

Located on the western coast north of Yaiza, Timanfaya National Park is the site of the famous volcanic eruptions that occurred in the 1700s. Covering 51 square kilometers in area, the surface of the national park is entirely made up of volcanic soil. As the surface temperature of the core fluctuates between 400° Celsius and 600° Celsius, volcanic activity continues to transpire beneath the surface. The park is named after the Timanfaya volcano, which has been documented as an active volcano even today. Access to the park is strictly regulated in order to protect the unique flora and fauna of the area and to ensure that tourists do not accidentally wander into the volcanic areas of the park.

Known for its unique Martian landscape, Timanfaya is a breathtaking glimpse at nature's power. You can take a coach trip around the National Park, the cost of which is included in the entry fee. You can also reserve a free guided walk by calling 48 hours in advance, or take a camel ride across the volcanic and picturesque landscape. The camels near the national park are cheaper compared to the ones on the road to the park, which can cost three times as much. Camel rides typically cost about €8 per person and include a picture of you while on the camel.

Upon entrance to the park, visitors are given a thrilling demonstration of just how hot the area is. Temperatures reach between 400° to 600° degrees Celsius just a few meters beneath the surface. Water poured onto the ground evaporates immediately, and water poured into a hole in the ground erupts seconds later in the form of a mini-geyser of steam. Dry brush thrown into that same hole catches fire immediately.

While you're there, be sure to visit "El Diablo Restaurant," which uses geothermal heat to cook its fare. There are few restaurants in the world that use a cast-iron grill placed over a large hole in the ground, so don't miss the opportunity to eat food cooked by a volcano! Visitors should know that the kitchen closes at 3 PM, so make sure to stop there early in the day.

Admission to the park is €8 per adult, which includes the coach tour fee. The coach bus drives through several high drop points and winding roads, hence if travelling in high seated coaches is not your cup of tea, taxis are available for hire at about €50 for a return trip. Another alternative is to rent a car and drive on your own. However, bear in mind that even the huge car parks available on site can get full during peak seasons. The park is open daily from 10 AM to 6 PM. For more information, call (+34) 928 84 00 57.

## Jardin de Cactus

Carretera General Del Norte,
Guatiza 35530
Tel: (+34) 928 52 93 97

http://www.visitcanaryislands.org/jardin-de-cactus-cactus-garden

Cactus plants thrive in the dry climate of Lanzarote, and in the northern area of Guatiza, over 10,000 different types of cactus plants thrive as proof. Developed under the guidance of island artist/architect Cesar Manrique, the cactus garden is one of the most popular attractions year-round.

The entire garden is a celebration of the world's spiniest plant, and each plant is displayed to their optimum effect against the backdrop of a stunning amphitheater hewn from an old quarry. The cactus theme is repeated in more than just the plants – door handles, wrought iron gates, and sculptures throughout the garden also sport cactus shapes.

Eminent botanist Estanislao Gonzales Ferrer headed up the plant selection, design, and layout of the garden. The impressive collection of cacti and other succulents hail from the Canary Islands, America, and Madagascar.

The cactus garden also gives visitors an opportunity to learn more about what was once the mainstay of a thriving Lanzarote industry. The Tuneri cactus attracts cochineal beetles. Their crushed larvae, once scraped from the plant, were once used to create a natural dye. Today, artificial dyes have replaced the cochineal beetle colorants, but since the cochineal dye is not toxic, it is still used in certain food and drink items.

The Tuneri cactus is just one of the thousands of species of cactus on display, and you'll be amazed at the incredible complexities and colors of cacti you encounter. During certain months in the year, various cactus plants sprout stunning flowers. After you've explored the garden, do stop for refreshments at the stylish bar located at the rear of the garden, beneath the restored Gofio mill. Serving light meals, snacks, tapas and sandwiches etc., the restaurant provides tourists lovely views across the cactus garden and of the windmills in the distance. The windmill is also accessible through a hilly path and for enthusiastic hikers, the windmill site promises outstanding views of the cacti garden below.

The cactus garden is open daily from 10 AM to 5:45 PM, and entrance fees are about €5 for adults, and €2.50 for children. If you get lost on your way to the garden, look up and locate an 8 meter high green metallic cactus statue that stands guard at the main entrance. If you plan to drive to the garden, hire a car in Lanzarote and drive to Guatiza in Teguise, taking the LZ-1 highway and take the Guatiza exist. The 8 meter high cactus also acts as an indicator from the main road and ensures that visitors do not miss the turn.

## Guinate Tropical Park & Penguin Paradise

http://www.guinatepark.com/

Established more than 20 years ago, the Guinate Tropical Park encompasses over 10 acres of land and is home to several tropical animals and birds. There are several modes of transport for those interested in exploring the park. Bus tours are the most inexpensive way to tour the park, but cars are also available for hire. Exploring the park, you can easily spend a few hours watching and interacting with lemurs, playful penguins and absolutely stunning macaws.

The park is home to several species of birds including and not restricted to cranes, penguins, ostriches, hornbills, macaws, finches, owls and toucans. The 3,200 square meter aviary, a beautiful and natural environment that houses these birds, also includes a lake called the Koi Carp Lake. Parrot shows, held at the Guinate Park Theater, are held throughout the day and last for about 25 minutes.

Penguins are housed in the Humboldt Penguin enclosure and gives the tourists a peek into the playful nature and behaviour of these adorable birds. Spectacular viewing panels allow the tourist to watch them in their natural habitats. Penguins are fed twice a day at 12 PM and 4 PM every day of the week except Thursdays. If lucky, you might even land an opportunity to help feed a penguin. Every enclosure in the park has supporting documentation detailing the species, their origin and their diet. Colourful maps and pictures make it informative and interesting for tourists of all ages.

While the park houses over 30 species of birds, animals aren't far behind. The Guinate Tropical Park boasts of an ever increasing assortment of mammals including and not restricted to the yellow mongoose, meerkats, wallabys, otters, lemurs and more. Because the species stay near their natural habitats, and Lanzarote enjoys temperate climates, there is continuous breeding of many species here at the park. If the timing is right, you might even be able to spot a young one being born and raised in the tropical park, so remember to bring your camera!

The tropical park is open all seven days of the week, from 10 AM to 5 PM. The entrance fee to the park costs about €14 per adult and about €6 per child aged 4 to 13 years old. Children aged 3 years or younger are admitted free. For any further information, call (+34) 928 83 55 00. If you plan to hire a car and drive down, take the northbound LZ-201 and drive up to the fork in the road which has a sign indicating the Guinate Tropical Park & Penguin Paradise on the left. Follow the signs to reach your destination.

## Jameos Del Agua

Carretera Orzola,
North of Arrieta,
Haría
http://www.turismolanzarote.com/en/detalle_centros.jsp?DS19.PROID=5102

Jameos Del Agua is an unusual attraction that is built out of a sheet of volcanic rock that is entirely underground. Designed by local artist and architect César Manrique, the underground entertainment complex includes a number of restaurants, cafes and shops below the surface of a tropical island beach. The complex is based on a unique geological formation developed by the artistic vision of Lanzarote's most famous son, Manrique. The Jameos Del Agua tourist center is also the very first tourist center designed by the architect and reflects his creative principles featuring a harmony between nature and Manrique's artistic creations.

Located inside a 6 kilometer tunnel created by the volcanic eruptions of La Corona Volcano, the Jameos Del Agua owes its name to a lake and is a most unusual geological formation. It was formed by water filtering over millennia through the rock that lies below sea level. The small entrance to the tunnel gives way to a spiral staircase created out of volcanic rock and wood and provides the first insight into the Jameo Chico, also known as the small Jameo. Ornamental elements and abundant vegetation fill the caves. Within the cave exists a natural lake with unbelievably clear water that is home to several endemic species, including the famed blind albino crabs which swim along the rocky floor of the caves. An interesting fact to note is that the lack of pigmentation in these barely one-centimeter crabs is due to the darkness within the grotto, which makes them whitish in colour. Also known as *jameitos*, these blind albino crabs are the symbol of Jameos Del Agua.

Beyond the caves, a small footbridge allows the visitor to cross the lake. The Big Jameo, or the Jameo Grande, lies beyond an ascending wall at the end of the footbridge. The volcanic grotto is home to a spectacular auditorium.

You can visit the Jameos Del Agua by bus or car trip. If you prefer to drive, take the northbound LZ-1 road and drive up to the fork that points to Jameos Del Agua on one side and Cueva de los Verdes on the other. Follow the signs to Jameos Del Agua.

Tours last for about an hour and the trip is priced at €9 per adult and €4.50 per child for children aged 7 to 12 years. Prices for residents of Canary Islands are cheaper and only cost €7.20 per adult and €3.60 per child. The complex is open Sundays to Fridays from 10 AM to 6:30 PM and on Saturdays from 10 AM to 10 PM. The Jameos Del Agua restaurant within the grotto is open from 11:30 AM to 4:30 PM while the café is open from 10 AM to 6:30 PM.

# Places to Stay

## Santa Rosa in Costa Teguise

Avda Del Mar 19, 35509 Costa Teguise
(+34) 928 09 02 42
http://www.lanzarote-tour.com/lanzarote/apartments/apartamentos_santa_rosa/santa_rosa.php
From $38 - $74/night

A Traveler's Choice 2012 winner, this hotel is a great place to stay whether you're on a romantic getaway or traveling with family. The hotel has a fitness center and restaurant, a swimming pool, and rooms come with kitchenettes. Free breakfast is offered in the mornings. The hotel is only a 10 minute walk from the nearest beach, and various restaurants and shops are situated nearby.

## Nautilus Bungalows in Puerto Del Carmen

Calle Gramillo 5, 35510 Puerto Del Carmen
(+34) 928 51 44 00
http://www.nautilus-lanzarote.com/lang/index.php
From $74/night

This quiet hotel is ideal for travelers of any age, and it includes room service and a restaurant, shuttle bus service, a swimming pool, and a bar/lounge. This is an excellent choice for those with disabilities as the owners have made an effort to make the hotel wheelchair accessible, with uniquely adapted bungalows for guests with special needs. They even have a special "casa del artista" which is a bungalow specially adapted to the needs of artists wishing to capture the views!

## Lancelot Hotel in Arrecife

Avenida Mancomunidad 9, 35500 Arrecife
(+34) 928 59 30 03
http://www.lanzarote.com/reservas/hotellancelot

From $59/night

The Lancelot hotel's helpful staff and clean rooms will make you feel right at home. The hotel is situated on the beach, and visitors can pay a little extra for a room with an ocean view. Hotel amenities include a swimming pool, gym and restaurant. The rooms are larger than average, and the breakfast buffet has received good reviews.

## Hotel Diamar in Arrecife

Avda. Fred Olsen 8, 35500 Arrecife
(+34) 928 81 56 65
http://www.hoteldiamar.es/presentaing.htm
From $61/night

Another charming hotel with an ocean view, amenities at this hotel include free high-speed internet, a restaurant and room service, and car rentals. Reducto beach is only a few steps away, and the city of Arrecife a few steps in the opposite direction. A little extra money will buy you a room with an ocean view, and you can watch the waves from your balcony as the sun sets.

## Jardines Del Sol

35570 Playa Blanca
http://jardinesdelsollanzarote.com/
From $59/night

The friendly and helpful staff at Jardines Del Sol aren't the only thing to recommend this hotel. Fully-fitted kitchens and flat-screen TVs with English-speaking channels make it a home away from home. Many bungalows include 2 bathrooms, ideal if you're traveling with your family. The hotel is also wheelchair accessible, making it ideal for those with disabilities. And feel free to play a game of chess on the giant chessboard located next to the pool!

# Eating & Drinking

## Restaurante El Navarro in Costa Teguise

Avenida Del Mar, 13, Costa Teguise

(+34) 928 59 21 45

Don't let looks deceive you - the average décor fades into the back of your mind as you sample some of the best food on the island. Feel free to walk in, but reservations are best, since the restaurant fills quickly on a nightly basis. This is the perfect place for a special dinner or late-night drink. Be prepared to pay a little more than average prices, but this is a restaurant that even travelers on a budget can afford to splurge on!

## TJ's Caribbean Tapas Bar in Puerto Del Carmen

8 Calle Teide, Old Town, 35510 Puerto Del Carmen
(+34) 689 81 58 06

This Caribbean restaurant is perfect for family meals or late-night drinks. The jerk chicken is famous, as well as the rum punch, and the owners Tony and Jeanette make visitors feel welcome. Expect good portions and fast service. Walk-ins are welcome, but reservations can also be made, and if you're there during the busy season, it may be a good idea to call ahead.

## Poppadom Indian Restaurant in Arrecife

Centro Comercial Maritimo, Local 9D, Avenida de Las Playas, 35510 Arrecife

(+34) 928 51 52 82
$13 - $36

The bustling city of Arrecife has dozens of highly recommended restaurants, but this multi-award winning Indian food chain is sure to hit the spot. It opened its doors in Arrecife in July of 2011, and has received rave reviews ever since. The extensive menu gives you a wide variety of choices, but if you'd like something you don't see, feel free to ask if it's available as the kitchen is very accommodating!

## Atlantico Bar Restaurant in Playa Blanca

Av. Papagayo no. 75 local 13, 35580 Playa Blanca
(+34) 656 97 30 60
https://www.facebook.com/AtlanticoRestaurant?sk=wall
$9 - $23

The seafood is best at this family-owned restaurant, and outdoor seating provides a view of the ocean. Things are quieter in the early evening—around 7 or 8 pm—if you're looking for a relaxed meal, but are open until 1 am most nights if you're looking for a late night eatery. Feel free to ask a local if you're having trouble finding it. The restaurant is located on the road behind the main group of restaurants on the sea front, opposite a church and above a Rental Car office.

## La Ermita Tapas Bar in Tias

Av. Central 57, 35572 Tias
(+34) 928 52 40 76
$9 - $23

This popular restaurant recommends that you get there early, or make reservations—they're usually full by 8 or 9 pm! Vegetarian options and a rich wine selection make the menu stand out from the rest, and visitors love the atmosphere.

# Shopping

## Calle Real in Arrecife

The capital city of Arrecife is the island's shopping center. The main shopping street is Calle Leon Y Castillo, the locals call the area Calle Real. Bazaars and retail shops sell a variety of goods from clothing to crafts. Prices are very reasonable, and considerably lower than those in major resorts. Many locations accept cash or card.

## Biosfera Shopping Center in Puerto Del Carmen

Overlooking the Old Town of Puerto del Carmen, this shopping mall is a great destination for clothes. Retailers like Pull and Bear, Levi's, Oyosho, Natural Shop, Crocs, Quicksilver, Pimkie, and Zara can all be found, in addition to an amusement arcade and several bars and restaurants. The mall is located on Calle Juan Carlos I, and is open Monday through Saturday from 10 am to 10 pm, with shortened hours on Sunday.

## Deiland Centre in Playa Honda

Another great mall, this indoor shopping center offers a combination of shops, services, and nightlife. Shops selling perfume, clothing, and gifts are all plentiful, as well as a supermarket, a cinema (Spanish only), and a bowling alley. The food court has several restaurants, including KFC and Burger King. Books and media shops make this mall complete.

## Old Capital Market in Costa Teguise

Every Sunday morning between 8:30 am and 2 pm, the old capital hosts an outdoor market. Hand-made tablecloths, jewelry, African wood carvings, local wines, paintings, and of course, knockoff watches and handbags can all be purchased from local vendors. When you tire of shopping, grab some paella or churros and watch the Canarian dancers in the main square, located in front of the Church. Haggling is expected.

## Casa-Museo Del Campesino in Mozaga

Most villages throughout the island have shops that sell pottery, basketwork, embroidery, jewelry and other traditional craft items. But the best place to find these items is at the Casa-Museo del Campesino. The museum serves as a monument and tribute to local farmers, and the gift shop is especially known for pottery made using the traditional techniques of hand-carving without a pottery wheel and firing pots in an open fire.

Printed in Great Britain
by Amazon